Belongs To
ELDER & CHI

THE BELIEVER'S GROWTH MANUAL

HELPING BELIEVERS DISCOVER THEIR POSITION IN CHRIST

ROBERT FREEMAN

JOSEPH A. ALEXANDER

215-778-6792

© 2003

Dominion Image Publications
(formally: IOGM Publications)
(www.estobi.com)

The Believer's Growth Manual
Helping Believers discover their position in Christ

Copyright © 2003 by Joseph A. Alexander

For information, address:
New Covenant Christian Ministries
1175 Boston Road
Bronx, NY 10456

ISBN: 0-9748875-0-1

Published by:
Dominion Image Publications
1167 Boston Road
Bronx, NY 10456
Tel: 718-617-0064

Cover art & page layout:
Timi Owobowale

Editorial services:
IOGM, Inc., USA

Except otherwise stated, all Scripture quotations are from the King James Version of the Bible.

Printed in the United States of America.

Dedication

This book is dedicated to all Church workers who have in various ways and times sought for simple material to help new Christians comprehend their newfound relationship. It is even for saints who have walked with the Lord for a long time but need to be refreshed so that they can help others. I pray that the content of this book will make your job easier and give you greater results.

Table Of Contents

Introduction

Salvation is a gift from God to you. You receive grace from God to be saved. Having been saved by grace, you are going to be kept by grace. As a child of God, you have an eternal relationship with God, which is sealed by the blood of Jesus Christ, and the Holy Spirit of God is a token evidence of that relationship. This was the reason the Lord revealed to the Apostle Paul to write the following for you.

And because of what Christ did, all (you others too), who heard the Good News about how to be saved, and trusted Christ, were marked as belonging to Christ by the Holy Spirit, who long ago had been promised to all of us Christians. His presence within us is God's guarantee that he really will give us all that he promised; and the Spirit's seal upon us means that God has already purchased us and that he guarantees to bring us to Himself. This is just one more reason to praise our Glorious God.
Ephesians 1:13-14, TLB

Your salvation was designed and approved by God. God seals you for eternity and nothing will be able to separate you from God. Based on this understanding, you need to approach God with a total commitment to know Him. Your goal must be to grow in the fullness of all that your heavenly Father has for you. Here's what the word of God has to say about the power of this relationship:

> Who dares accuse us whom God has chosen for His own? Will God? No! He is the one who has forgiven us and given us right standing with himself. Who then will condemn us? Will Christ? No! For He is the one who died for us and came back to life again for us, and is sitting at the place of highest honor next to God, pleading for us there in heaven. Who then can ever keep Christ's love from us? **Romans 8:33-35a, TLB**

Your salvation has a full guarantee by God. Therefore, move forward to know your God and walk with Him through eternity.

A Personal Note

Dear Friend,

I rejoice in the fact that you have trusted the Lord Jesus as your personal Savior. The Bible says, "Therefore, if any man be in Christ, he is a new creature: old things are passed away; behold all things are become new" (II Corinthians 5:17).

You can live a victorious Christian life. You do not have to be a defeated Christian. The Lord will forgive you of your sins each day and strengthen you *if* you are willing to obey Him and walk in His way. "If we confess our sins, He is faithful and just to forgive us our sins, and to cleanse us from all unrighteousness" (I John 1:9).

The material in this booklet is designed to help you understand more about what it means to be a Christian. These simple lessons will also help you get started in the right direction as you begin your new life as a Christian. They are given to you with a prayer that you will let our wonderful Lord bless and use you like He wants to.

May the Lord strengthen and build you in His might and power.

Joseph A. Alexander

A Few Things To Remember

Your Christian journey has just begun; know, however, that you are not alone in this blessed journey. Others have gone this way before you. They have experienced great victory, and you too can, and will enjoy the same.

The Church and other believers want to be of help to you in your walk with the Lord. It is important that you avail yourself of their support. You may do this by speaking to the pastor, the deacons or deaconesses, or any recognized spiritual leader in your local church. Do your best to identify these people early in your walk with Christ. Remember, the telephone number of your church is available for you to contact your church leaders when necessary.

Let me dispel your doubt from the start. Many people have various misconceptions about the Church; consequently, they enter the church with doubt. Ultimately, doubt also keeps them from benefiting from the genuine counsel, support and helps found in the church. Their greatest fears are being taken advantage of, being hurt by others, etc. In any living church family, I want to guarantee you that, by God's grace, there are saints who have learned to become all things to all people.

Be assured of this one thing: the people of God care about you and want to see you grow in Christ. Furthermore, the pastor cares and would like to counsel and assist you in developing your relationship with the Lord.

Things To Remember Each Day

1. You are saved forever.

2. Your salvation is a fact based on faith, not a feeling.

3. You are now a child of God.

4. If you sin, ask your Heavenly Father to forgive and cleanse you, because He guaranteed that He would (see I John 1:8-9).

5. Read your Bible regularly and spend time in prayer.

6. Yield and submit yourself to God's control by the power of the Holy Spirit.

7. Obey God's Word.

8. Remain in regular fellowship with your church family.

9. Support your church consistently with your tithes, offerings (and gifts of the Holy Spirit in you).

10. Tell others about Jesus Christ and how they too can be saved.

CHAPTER ONE

What Does It Mean To Be Saved?

Many people are confused about what it means to be saved or to be a Christian. Let's look to the Word of God for clarity. The Bible says there is a heaven (see John 14:1-6); and there is a hell (see Luke 16:19-31, Revelation 21:8). The only way to get to heaven and miss hell is to have Christ in your heart.

So the next question is, "How can I get Christ into my heart?" It is by personal invitation and acceptance of Him as your personal Savior. Romans 10:9-10 tell us exactly what to do and the word of God is true forever. Trusting in Jesus Christ alone is the only way He can save us from hell and take us to heaven.

Realize This One Thing: God Loves You

For God so loved the world, that He gave His only

begotten Son, that whosoever believeth in Him should not perish, but have everlasting life. **John 3:16**

We were all born in sin regardless of ethnicity, socioeconomic status, religious background, political affiliations or physical attributes. Sin became a part of us at birth. Thus, all of us are sinners in need of grace, regardless of color, race, education or position in life. The Word of God states that, "...All have sinned, and come short of the glory of God" (Romans 3:23). We are condemned without Christ (see John 3:18). What does that mean? It means that without Christ, we are spiritually dead and headed for hell (see Ephesians 2:12).

Our Sins Must Be Paid For

"For the wages of sin is death; ..." (Romans 6:23). The payment of our sins is death and hell. But the good news of the gospel is life and peace.

Christ Paid For Our Sins

...and while we were yet sinners, Christ died for us. **Romans 5:8**

The Lord Jesus came from heaven. He was born of a virgin (see Luke 1:26-28). He lived a sinless life (see Hebrews 4:15). He owed debt of sin, meaning He was born without the original sin that afflicts every person born by a woman. Yet, He went to the cross for us where He took all our sins on Himself (see I Timothy 1:15; 2:5-6). Then He was buried and rose from the dead on the third day (see I Corinthians 15:1-6).

We Must Ask Him By Faith To Save Us

For whosoever shall call upon the name of the Lord shall be saved" (Romans 10:13). We know Christ died for our sins and desires to save us, but we must ask Him to do so—He promised He would. The moment you ask Him, Christ comes into your heart, forgives your sins, and saves your soul. He then writes your name in the Book of Life (see Revelation 21:27). You become a new creature (see II Corinthians 5:17). You become a child of God (see John 1:12).

Questions and Answers

Question: Jesus saves you from what?

Answer: Jesus saves you from your sins (Mark 2:11, Matthew 26:28).

Question: What is sin?

Answer: Sin is disobedience to God or breaking the Law of God (I John 3:4).

Question: Who has sinned?

Answer: We have all sinned against God (Romans 3:10, 23).

Question: What is the penalty for your sin?

Answer: The penalty is eternal death in hell (Romans 6:23).

Question: How can I be saved from this death?

Answer: You can be saved from eternal death by trusting Jesus Christ as your Savior (Acts 16:31).

Bible Study Assignment

1. Read John chapter 5 in the New Testament. Take time to read the entire chapter carefully.

2. Reread the same chapter. This time note the verses which talk about eternal life and how we can be sure God gives us this life through the Lord Jesus Christ.

Bible Memory Verse

Assurance of Salvation

These things have I written unto you that believe on the name of the Son of God; that ye may know that ye have eternal life, and that ye may believe on the name of the   Son of God. **I John 5:13**

Consider the Living Bible translation of the same verse:

I have written this to you who believe in the Son of God so that you may know you have eternal life. **I John 5:13, TLB**

As a new believer or a young Christian, there are several things you must do in your new position in

Christ. Among them is memorizing the scriptures. There is absolutely nothing else that will help you to mature in Christ more than the Word of God. The truth is, you are going to face challenges, both from your adversary (referred to in the Bible as Satan) and your old self. Put in biblical language, you are going to be engaged in "spiritual warfare."

However, do not panic or be afraid: you are an overcomer since you are born into the family of the great Champion of all ages—Jesus Christ, your Lord.

Later on in our study, we shall discuss one of the strategies for victory—**a time-proven method that has never, and will never fail in the life of any child of God.**

CHAPTER TWO

What Does It Mean To Be Baptized?

The Lord Jesus Christ founded the New Testament Church. He said, "...upon this rock I will build my Church..." (Matthew 16:18). The Bible further states, "...Christ also loved the church, and gave himself for it" (Ephesians 5:25).

Christ gave what we call doctrines and ordinances to the Church. The doctrines of the Church are its beliefs and teachings. The ordinances of the Church are the things He instructed us to observe. They are called ordinances because He commanded or ordered that they be obeyed. In the New Testament Church, there are two ordinances—one is baptism while the other is the Lord's Supper (or communion).

The Lord's Supper was instituted by our Savior, Jesus Christ, the night He was betrayed and delivered to die for our sins on the cross. No one is saved by partaking of the Lord's Supper. It is a memorial of the death of the Lord Jesus Christ; a reminder of what He did for us on the cross. Those who have trusted the Lord Jesus as their Savior and have followed Him in baptism may partake of the Lord's Supper. The Lord's Supper is an ordinance given to the Church by our Lord Himself to represent His flesh and His blood offered to us at Calvary. The bread represents the body of the Lord which was broken on the cross and given as life sustenance to the believer.

While He was on earth Jesus had said to the Jews in John 6, "I am the bread of life, he that cometh to me shall never hunger (verse 35), " I am the bread of life" (verse 48), "This is the bread which cometh down from heaven, that a man may eat thereof, and not die" (verse 50). Again He said, "I am the living bread which came down from heaven: if any man eat of this bread, he shall live for ever: and the bread that I will give is my flesh, which I will give for the life of the world" (verse 51).

The wine (fruit of the vine or grape juice depending upon where you are in the world) represents the Lord's blood. He had said to the Jews of his day, "Verily, verily, I say unto you, Except ye eat the flesh of the Son of man, and drink his blood, ye have no life in you" (verse 53). *Therefore, the Lord's Supper (bread and wine or grape juice), symbolizes the Lord's broken body and blood given for us.* These can be called *type* and *symbols* in the teaching of the Church. They are a representation of the real. The real thing is Jesus Christ Himself.

What Is Baptism A Type Of?

Baptism is a type of burial and resurrection. We are buried with Christ in the likeness of His death; and we are raised in the likeness of His resurrection (see Romans 6:1-4). Both of these ordinances of the Church are beautiful pictures of spiritual truth, yet they have no saving power. They only picture what the Lord Jesus has done for us.

Baptism pictures the death, burial and resurrection of Jesus Christ our Lord. It also pictures our sin and the new life we have in Christ. It is a public declaration of what has already taken place in our hearts. It tells others that we believe that the Lord Jesus died for us, was buried for us, and arose from the dead for us. It also tells them that we have invited Him into our hearts as our personal Savior and we are no longer lost, but have new life in Him.

Who Is Baptism For?

Remember that baptism is for believers only, therefore, you must be saved before you can be baptized. Acts 2:41 is an important scripture where Peter helped the Jews of his time to see the necessity of baptism. Acts 8:37 is another scripture that will help you understand that this experience is for believers only. Also, remember that in baptism, we are obeying Christ, and not man or tradition. In His final words, the Lord Jesus said we are to be baptized after we are saved (see Matthew 28:19-20).

How Should We Be Baptized?

The Bible teaches that we are to be baptized by immersion; that is, being buried in water. It means going under the water and coming up out of the water. Please note that Jesus our Lord Himself was baptized this way (see Matthew 3:16). The New Testament Church also baptized in the same way (see Acts 8:38). In Paul's epistle to the Romans, we are instructed that baptism is a burial, implying going under the water or being immersed in the water (see Romans 6:2-4).

As we stand in the water, the water crossing our

body is a picture of the cross where Jesus died. Going beneath the water is a picture of how Jesus went into the grave. Coming out of the water is a picture of how Jesus came out of the grave alive forever.

What If I Was Baptized By Sprinkling, Should I Be Baptized Again?

Since baptism is an act of obedience to the Word of the Lord, I believe that what is worth doing should be done right. Obedience must be complete or it is not obedience. Therefore, if you were sprinkled, and now you discover that the Bible says that you should be immersed, it is only proper for you to do what the Bible teaches. Total obedience satisfies the good conscience.

Questions And Answers

Question: Who baptized Jesus?

Answer: John the Baptist did (Matthew 3:13-16).

Question: Where was Jesus baptized?

Answer: Jesus was baptized in the Jordan River (Matthew 3:13-14).

Question: Why was Jesus baptized since He did not have to repent of any sin?

Answer: Jesus was baptized to fulfill all righteousness and as evidence of total obedience to God the Father (Matthew 3:15).

Question: What is baptism?

Answer: Baptism is a symbol that represents the burial and resurrection of Jesus Christ (Colossians 2:12).

Question: What is the meaning of baptism?

Answer: Baptism pictures three things (Romans 6:23, Galatians 3:27).

1. It pictures the death, burial and resurrection of Jesus Christ

2. It pictures our death to sin and our resurrection to a new life in Christ.

3. It pictures our faith that when we die and are buried in Christ, we shall also be raised from the dead as Christ did.

Question: Did Jesus command us to be baptized?

Answer: Yes. According to His Great Command or commission in Matthew 28:18-20, all who accept Jesus as their Savior are to be baptized.

Facts About The Bible That Every Believer Should Know

1. *The Bible is the Word of God.*

All scripture is given by inspiration of God, and is profitable for doctrine, for reproof, for correction, for instruction in righteousness: that the man (or child) of God may be perfect, thoroughly furnished unto all good works. **II Timothy 3:16-17 (emphasis added)**

2. *God used human beings to write the Bible for us.*

Knowing this first, that no prophecy of the scripture is of any private interpretation. For the prophecy came not in old time by the will of man: but holy men of God spake as they were moved by the Holy Spirit. **II Peter 1:20-21**

CHAPTER THREE

The Bible In The Believer's Life

The new Christian must let God speak to his/her heart and direct his/her life. God speaks to us through the Bible and, through prayer, we speak to God. Let us consider the Bible, the Word of God, for a moment in our preparation to take our rightful position in Christ.

The Bible

The Bible is the most amazing book. It is actually a library of sixty-six (66) books put together as one. There is the Old Testament, having thirty-nine (39) books, beginning with the book of Genesis and ending with the book of Malachi. And there is the New Testament, having twenty-seven (27) books, beginning with the book of Matthew and ending with the book of Revelation. There are 1189 chapters in the Bible. Nine hundred and twenty-nine (929) are in the Old Testament, and two hundred and sixty (260) in the New Testament.

By reading four (4) chapters a day, one can read through the entire Bible in less than a year. Determine to read your Bible through at least once each year. The best time of the day for Bible reading and prayer is in the early morning. Make it a habit to rise early and begin the day with God.

What To Know As A Fact

The Bible answers the three greatest questions man will ever ask:

1. Where did I come from?

2. Why am I here?

3. Where am I going?

Of greatest importance is that the Bible has one theme, and that is: the Lord Jesus Christ—Savior, Deliverer and Friend.

Conclusion

Memorize God's Word and hide it in your heart. The Bible says in Psalm 119:11, "Thy word have I hid in my heart, that I might not sin against Thee."

CHAPTER FOUR

Prayer In The Believer's Life

The Lord Jesus provides a prime example of a life of prayer. He got up early in the morning and spent time in prayer. He regularly left the crowds to spend time alone with the Father in prayer. Prayer becomes more effective in the life of the believer as he/she prays more often and at specified times.

The prayer life of a new Christian may begin slow and very simple, but a Christian who does not pray is certain to fail in some areas. Set aside certain times of the day to pray. Pray on your knees when you can, as you arise in the morning and at your bedside before you retire at night. Pray before taking your meals whether you are in public or private places.

Ask God in prayer to meet your needs, to give you strength, and to save your loved ones, friends, and neighbors. Get close to the Lord through prayer. Remember that prayer is an intimate sharing of our heart with God. Don't be afraid to make a mistake in prayer. God is interested in your heart rather than your eloquence. Do not imitate others.

Memory Verses To Help You

If ye abide in Me, and My words abide in you, ye shall ask what ye will, and it shall be done unto you. **John 15:17**

Call unto me, and I will answer thee, and shew thee great and mighty things, which thou knowest not. **Jeremiah 33:3**

And this is the confidence that we have in Him, that, if we ask any thing according to His will, He heareth us: And if we know that He hears us, whatsoever we ask, we know that we have the petitions that we desired of Him. **I John 5:14,15**

Be careful for nothing; but in every thing by prayer and supplication with thanksgiving let your requests be made known unto God. And the peace of God, which passeth all understanding, shall keep your hearts and minds through Christ Jesus. **Philippians 4:6,7**

Ask, and it shall be given you, seek, and ye shall

find; knock, it shall be opened unto you: For everyone that asked receiveth; and he that seeketh findeth; and to him that knocketh it shall be opened. **Matthew 7:7,8**

CHAPTER FIVE

The New Christian & His/Her Local Church

The Universal Family Of God

When you receive the Lord Jesus into your heart, you are saved. You automatically become a part of God's eternal family. This family is universal. Everyone in the world who is born again by the Spirit of God belongs to the family of God. However, when you obey the Lord Jesus Christ in baptism, you become a member of that local Church or family of believers.

The Local Family Of God

A local Church, then, can be called a group of baptized believers who obey the Lord and, by His direction, joined themselves voluntarily to carry out the plans and the purposes of God on earth. In addition to many other things, the greatest call of this group of believers is to fulfill what we call the *great command* or the *great commission*.

The other responsibility of this group is to worship, fellowship, and encouraging one another to do the primary work, which is to lead people to Christ and advance His kingdom on earth.

What is the Great Commission?

In Matthew 28:19-20, our Lord said:

Go ye therefore, and teach all nations, baptizing them in the name of the Father, and of the Son, and of the Holy Ghost: Teaching them to observe all things whatsoever I have commanded you: lo, I am with you always, even unto the end of the world. Amen.

Look at some very important steps in this wonderful command of the Lord to His followers in their order as follows:

FIRST – we are to go to people. Some churches seem to believe that we are just to announce our services and wait for people to come to us. The Lord Jesus said, "GO!"

SECOND – we are to explain to those that we go to how they can be saved. We must tell them in clear, unbiased, simple terms how they can be saved or come to know and accept the Lord Jesus Christ as their personal Savior.

THIRD – after they are saved or have accepted the Lord Jesus, they are to be baptized in a local church as an act of obedience to the commandment of Christ their Lord and Savior.

FOURTH – the Church is to teach the new Christian the things that Christ has instructed us to teach in His Word. This means that the new Christian is to be faithful in attending church services, so that he/she may worship regularly with God's people, particularly, in Bible study. He or she will grow and develop, the way a true Christian ought to as he/she faithfully hears the Word of God being proclaimed.

The Importance Of The Local Church

The Bible says that the Lord Jesus Christ founded the Church and loves the Church, which is His body.

> ...and upon this rock I will build my church; and the gates of hell shall not prevail against it.
> **Matthew 16:18**

...Christ also loved the Church, and gave himself for it. **Ephesians 5:25**

We can see that the Church is neither a human institution nor did it originate from man. The local pastor or the bishop only serves under Christ. Jesus Christ founded the Church and He is the Head of the Church. In another scripture, He is called the Bridegroom and the Church is His bride (see Matthew 25:1-13).

What Each Christian Can Do For His/Her Church

We often think a lot about what the Church can do in ministering to others, but we also need to think about what church members can do for their church. With some measure of priority, I have summarized the following as some of the things that I believe all Christians should do for their church.

Pray For Your Church

The Church of Jesus Christ faces challenging attacks daily from the enemy of Christ. No other institution on earth has been given the authority to plunder Satan's kingdom besides the Church. Therefore, the Church is always under the attack of the adversary. Each member of the Church then needs to ask the Lord to meet the needs of their local body and that of the body of Christ at large.

Pray for the leaders. Pray that everything the Church does will be pleasing to the Head of the Church, which is Christ. Pray that the Church will be diligent in fulfilling the great command and the commission of the Master.

In Ephesians chapter 6 verses 18-20, the Apostle Paul helps us to understand the need to pray for the Church, teachers, and missionaries in the field to speak the Word of God boldly.

Be A Loyal Member

Loyalty encourages both the pastor and the leadership of the Church. The Bible encourages all members of the Church to show themselves as dependable to the leadership. Encourage other members of the Church to be loyal as well. Do not complain, if you have a need; seek the right person in the leadership to help you.

If you need to know something about your church,

ask. That is why God has raised leaders—to help you function effectively in the Body (the Bible calls the Church the *Body of Christ*).

People who complain are called murmurers. They are the major hindrance to growth and progress in the Church. If you recall the story of those who left Egypt with Moses, you will see that they started complaining and caused the entire nation of Israel to wander in the wilderness for forty years when the journey could have been accomplished in eleven days!

See what the scripture says: "Neither murmur ye as some of them also murmured, and were destroyed of the destroyer" (I Corinthians 10:10). See also Jude verse 16 for further reference.

Be A Faithful Member

Faithfulness is observable and can be measured by one's actions. As a faithful member of your church, you should attend the scheduled worship and teaching services regularly. This is very important because attending the scheduled services establishes faithfulness, and attending them faithfully brings definite benefits that can be categorized as follows:

1. It is obeying what the Bible teaches.

2. It identifies you publicly with the Lord and His people.

3. It provides instruction for living the Christian life.

4. It helps you locate God's will in a place of service.

5. It makes you a part of getting the message of salvation to others.

If it were not for Bible-preaching churches, many people would not hear how to be saved, including you.

Support Your Church

It is God's plan for each member of the Church to be a tither. That means we are to give a tenth or ten percent (10%) of our income to the Lord. The tenth is not tax, but an act of obedience and appreciation. We should also give an offering above our tithe, which is an obligation for complete blessing according to the teaching of God's Word (see Malachi 3:6-10).

In I Corinthians 16:2, the Bible says, "Upon the first day of the week (which is our day of worship or Sunday) let every one of you lay by him (or her) in store, as God hath prospered him (or her), that there be no gatherings when I come" (emphasis added). This scripture is very important as it clearly states that your giving is based upon what you earn from work or investments (as God has prospered you).

With a heart of gratitude, as a member of the local Church, you should do all you can to make your Church all it ought to be.

This kind of gracious, voluntary, and obedient giving will help the Church to fulfill all that God intended the Church to do in supporting the poor, in sending the Gospel to the ends of the earth, and in taking care of those who serve in the ministry of the Church or the body of Christ. The Pastor, who is the Shepherd, will be taken care of also according to the Word of God.

CHAPTER SIX

The New Christian & Soul Winning

Memory Verses To Consider As We Examine The Issue Of Soul Winning In The Life Of The New Christian:

The fruit of the righteous is a tree of life; and he that winneth souls is wise. **Proverbs 11:30**

And they that be wise shall shine as the brightness of the firmament; and they that turn many to righteousness as the stars forever and ever. **Daniel 12:3**

Let him know that he which converteth the sinner from the error of his way shall save a soul from death and shall hide a multitude of sins. **James 5:20**

The delight and joy of every Christian should be

to tell unbelievers about Jesus Christ, their Savior, and then see them accept Him and become saved from the power of Satan.

It is very hard to describe this experience because we could not comprehend it while we were still in our sins. Now, that our eyes have been opened, we can look back and see what great things the Lord has done for us. You see, to have an eternal relationship with the Father is the greatest joy anyone can have on earth. That is why we desire to see others have this joy.

This fact must be clearly understood. Everyone must receive Jesus Christ as their personal Savior in order to get to heaven. To put it plainly, unless a person is saved (that is, to accept Jesus as personal Lord and Savior), such a person belongs to Satan. Let's look at the condition of all unsaved persons on earth to clarify this further.

The Unsaved Person's Condition
According To The Bible

1. They are completely lost (Luke 19:10).

2. The direction of their lives is away from God (Isaiah 53:63).

3. They are perishing in their sins (John 3:16).

4. They are condemned along with the Devil already (John 3:18).

5. They are, along with the Devil, under the wrath of God (John 3:36).

6. They are blind and are being led by the enemy of their soul (II Corinthians 4:3-6).

7. They are without hope in this world and in the world that is to come (Ephesians 2:17).

8. They are spiritually dead because of their sin (Ephesians 2:1).

9. They are missing life's best, which God in Christ came to provide for them (John 10:10).

10. They will spend eternity in an awful place called **HELL** that has been prepared for the Devil and his angels (Matthew 25:41).

We Are Commanded To Tell The Lost How To Be Saved

Let us be genuine with ourselves and honest with the Lord who has saved us. It is a fact that we all are beneficiaries of another person's care. By that I mean someone cared enough about those of us who are now Christians to tell us how to be saved. Someone prayed for us consistently and then took the initiative to approach us about Christ or invited us to a church or a meeting where we made our confession and received Jesus Christ as our Savior. So it is of necessity that we also tell others.

Most importantly, the Lord Jesus Christ commanded us to go and tell others how to be saved (see Matthew 28:19-20). Our burden for the lost should increase as we go after them for Christ. Our love for Jesus Christ should also increase as we learn to obey Him by following His most urgent command: "Go ye."

Where Do We Begin?

The best people to start witnessing to are our loved ones. Every Christian should immediately start telling their family members about Jesus Christ and His saving power. The next set of people is our co-workers at our places of employment, or fellow students, for those who are in school. As you can see, you begin sharing your faith with those who are close to you; who knew you before Jesus completed the work of grace in your life.

Remember That Christ Is The One Who Can Save The Lost

There is no one so lost or wretched that Christ Jesus cannot save. He will save anyone who calls upon Him for salvation. The assurance for this position is found in the Bible itself because in Romans 10:13, the Word of God says: **"For whosoever shall call upon the name of the Lord shall be saved."**

He will also help us talk to others about being saved. It is the will of God that we do this consistently. Therefore, the Holy Spirit of God will give us the strength and the boldness to witness as we move forward by faith to obey Christ.

How Do We Begin To Witness?

The best way to begin witnessing is by giving your personal testimony. Your testimony tells of your personal experience; what happened to you and/or what you received. Accordingly, we can start witnessing by testifying about what Christ has done for us. A Christian's testimony calls attention to four significant things:

1. My life before receiving Christ.

2. How I came to know Christ.

3. What happened to me after receiving Christ?

4. What Christ means to me since I have been saved.

The most important thing we need to bear in mind is our genuineness. Our faith in Christ and our personal salvation are real. People are looking for a way out of their misery, but they will not admit or cry to the Savior who can deliver them because the 'god' of this world has blinded their eyes.

Therefore, do not be alarmed when people pretend that they do not need Jesus Christ. Your duty and mine is to tell them about the love of Jesus Christ, and what that love can do for them in their present state of sin and hopelessness.

Conclusion

As we end this chapter, realize that fear is a natural human feeling when we begin to witness. Witnessing is a spiritual action and we must depend upon the Holy Spirit. We can overcome our fears. When we are afraid, we must trust in God. After all, witnessing and soul winning are things that we must ask God to help us accomplish.

Remember one thing; the Lord will use you to help change the course of another's eternal destiny as you tell them how to be saved. You are not the one doing the changing; God is only using you to do so. Please be very conscious of this one thing: the Holy Spirit is waiting all the time to use you. Now, since He wants to use you, why not let the Lord do the work through you? Be bold and be strong in the power of His might.

Memory Verse

And He said unto them, Go ye into all the world, and preach the gospel to every creature. **Mark 16:15**

How to Get Started?

Soul winning calls for action on the part of the Christian. You cannot just wait and hope that it will happen. The first thing to do is begin praying. Create a list of friends, family members, co-workers and other loved ones that you want to see saved.

Use the space below to list the names of the people you are praying for. Ask others in the church or your prayer group to join you in prayer.

My Personal Prayer List:

1. _____
_____

2. _____
_____

3. _____
_____

4. _____
_____

5. _____
_____

6. _____
_____

7. _____
_____

8. _____
_____

9. _____
_____

10. _____
_____

Helpful Scriptures To Memorize

For by grace are ye saved through faith; and that
not of yourselves: it is the gift of God: not of works,
lest any man should boast. **Ephesians 2:8-9**

And you, being in your sins and the un-
circumcision of your flesh, hath He quickened
together with Him, having forgiven you all
trespasses. **Colossians 2:13**

Blotting out the handwriting of ordinances that was
against us, which was contrary to us, and took it
out of the way, nailing it to His cross. **Colossians
2:14**

And having spoiled principalities and powers, He
made a show of them openly, triumphing over them
in it. **Colossians 2:15**

CHAPTER SEVEN

The Holy Spirit &
The New Christian

The Christian life is the greatest life that is offered to any human on Earth. God has given us the most fantastic promises. However, it is a shame that many of us are only dreaming about the realization of these precious promises of God. Consider such promises recorded in John's Gospel:

> ...and If any man thirst, let him come unto me, and drink. He that believeth on me, as the scripture hath said, out of his belly shall flow rivers of living water. **John 7:37-38**

The Word of God goes on to say in the next verse that Jesus spoke these words concerning the Holy Spirit, which they that believe on Him should receive.

Note: the Spirit was not yet given because Christ was not yet glorified.

The Holy Spirit

The natural question that will come to a new believer's mind is, "Who then, is the Holy Spirit? What is He supposed to do? How do I receive Him since the Holy Spirit is a gift? How can He help me in my Christian walk in this world?"

These are the questions that I hope to help you answer in this chapter.

Who Is The Holy Spirit?

The Word of God must be the basis of all learning about the Holy Spirit. According to Jesus in one of His teachings and admonitions to the disciples, the Lord called the Holy Spirit the promise of the Father - read Luke 24:49. However, in general terms, the Holy Spirit is a personality the same way Jesus and the Father are personalities within the Godhead. The Holy Spirit is the third person of the Trinity. Therefore, the Holy Spirit is God.

A term such as the TRINITY might be difficult for you to comprehend at this time. My advice to you is not to worry about the terminologies, but to follow the scriptures carefully for the Word of God will explain itself.

In the Bible, we are told that the Holy Spirit is the giver of power to accomplish the plan of God. Our Lord, in speaking to the disciples before His final departure said:

> But ye shall receive power, after that the Holy Ghost is come upon you: and ye shall be witnesses unto me both in Jerusalem, and in all Judea, and in Samaria, and unto the uttermost part of the earth. **Acts 1:8**

So the Holy Spirit gives power to believers to enable them witness or accomplish the plan of God. Jesus Christ also calls Him, the Comforter.

> ...and He (the Father) shall give you another Comforter, that He may abide with you forever; Even the Spirit of Truth whom the world cannot receive; because it seeth Him not... **John 14:16-17**

The Holy Spirit is also a Guide and a Counselor to the believer. Jesus said:

> Howbeit, when he, the Spirit of truth is come, he will guide you into all truth: for he shall not speak of himself; but whatsoever he shall hear (from Me), that shall he speak: and He will shew you things to come. **John 16:13 (emphasized)**

What Is He Supposed To Do?

Another way to say this question could be, "Why do we need the Holy Spirit?" Whichever way it is phrased, the question is very important. Jesus once said, "He that believeth on me, the works that I do shall he do also; and greater works than these shall he do; because I go unto my Father. And whatsoever ye shall ask in my name, that will I do..." (John 14:12-13)

We have to accept the fact that we cannot do anything of substance in the Kingdom of God without the power of the Holy Spirit. We do not have the power in and of ourselves to accomplish these works that Jesus speaks of. We can only move supernaturally as we are filled with Holy Spirit or as Christ comes and lives within us to work through our hands, speak through our lips, and love through our lives, to do the primary work and carry out the will of God. That is why Jesus said, "But you shall receive power, after that the Holy Ghost is come upon you..." (Acts 1:8a) Just let Him come upon you so that you can accomplish great things for the honor of God.

Many Christians do not understand the importance of approaching the Holy Spirit by faith and allow-ing Him to work through them. As a new Christian, you need to rely on Him by faith to fill and use you.

Let us return to the question of "What is the Holy Spirit supposed to do in the life of a believer?" His work is to fill the believer and glorify God through the life of the believer. It is a fact that without Christ, we can do nothing of substance in the Kingdom of God or impact Satan's kingdom. The Holy Spirit then is the Enabler or the Helper of the Christian. He is the Producer of fruits within the branch of the Vine, Christ Jesus.

How Do You Receive The Holy Spirit?

The Holy Spirit is called a "Gift". Jesus also called Him "the Promise of the Father" and "another Comforter". When we examine all three descriptive names of Holy Spirit, you will notice that they point to His work in us when we receive Him. Remember that the Holy Spirit is a person. This is a clear revelation of God in the Bible—Jesus himself taught us.

As a gift, the Holy Spirit must be received. When anyone is given a gift, to have the full benefit of the gift so designated, the intended receivers must acknowledge the gift. As a Christian, the Holy Spirit is

THE BELIEVER'S GROWTH MANUAL

given as a gift to you. All you have to do is open your heart and receive Him. Please do not make it complicated for yourself; God has already given the gift to you because you believe in Jesus Christ.

Jesus said, "He that believeth in Me...out of His belly, shall flow rivers of living water" (John 7:38). He spoke of the Holy Spirit that believers would receive. The Holy Spirit is also called "Another Comforter". The term 'another' implies that there was one before this one.

We can ascertain that the first Comforter must be Jesus Christ Himself. The question one can ask is, "How do you receive Jesus Christ?" As a Christian, you can answer that without much trouble because you have received Christ as your Savior. He forgave all your sins and made you a new creature in Himself. Well, you received Christ by faith. You asked Him to come into your heart because you believed in His finished work on Calvary. Having believed in Him, you confessed with your mouth and you were saved.

Since the Holy Spirit is a "Comforter" like Jesus Christ, you can equally receive Him by faith. How? Believe in your heart and confess Him with your mouth, because Jesus Christ has already sent Him into the world—He is here. Before, the Holy Spirit was a promise, but we have a well-documented record that He came on the day of Pentecost. Read the book of Acts of the Apostles chapter 2:1-13.

The evidence of His work is very clear in your life because you are saved. Without the Holy Spirit, you would not have been saved. Conviction is the work of the Holy Spirit. No human being can be saved without being convicted of sin. You should remember the same way that I do, that one day the Holy Spirit convicted you, then pointed you to Jesus Christ, who you received by faith and became saved. Examine the following scriptures for yourself: John 3:5, 14:16, 16:13-14 and I Corinthians 3:16.

How Can The Holy Spirit Help Me?

God knows that you could not live the Christian life to any successful degree without His help. Note very carefully, that becoming a child of God through Christ was God's design or His plan. Sometimes we make the mistake of thinking that we got ourselves saved after we tried everything else, then finally decided to try Jesus and be saved. This is incorrect. God initiated our salvation and has made adequate preparation to give us the Holy Spirit who will help us to live a victorious and accomplishing life for Him. Our lives do not belong to us nor do we serve ourselves. Read II Corinthians 5:14-16 pay specific attention to verse 15 the statement "that they which live should not henceforth live unto themselves, but unto Him, which died for them and rose again".

What Does It Mean To Be Filled With The Holy Spirit?

The Word of God admonishes us to be filled with the Holy Spirit. Another word for filling could be controlled. So we can say that to be filled by the Holy Spirit is to be controlled by Him. In Ephesians 5:18, the Apostle Paul used the term "be filled with the Spirit". If you look at this verse you will notice that he first instructed the believer not to be drunk with wine or liquor but rather with the Holy Spirit.

Following the Apostle's illustrative thought, a drunkard is under the total influence of liquor, which has taken over his or her body. In modern terminology, the "spirit" created by the dominance of a substance (wine, liquor, etc.) is in control of the man or woman who has so willingly submitted themselves to that substance.

We can go on to say that the body of the individual has been fully saturated by the "spirit" or the "substance". Therefore, the actions or responses of the person when under such control are not theirs but that which is generated or created by the "substance".

Equally, we can say that to be filled with the Holy Spirit of God, which the scripture instructs us to be, means that we are no longer under the control of ourselves, but the Spirit of God is. He empowers or generates within us the desires of God so that our actions or responses are no longer ours, but that of the Holy Spirit.

With this understanding, we can now move forward to see how our lives must be submitted to the Holy Spirit of God. It is important to know that the same way in which a drunkard willingly takes in his wine; believers must willingly submit themselves to the Holy Spirit. The key word that we must understand here is "FILLED". When a believer is filled with the Holy Spirit, who is the third person in the Godhead (please note that He is not a force), He controls that vessel (the believer) as God's vessel to glorify God.

The Gifts Of The Holy Spirit

The gifts of the Holy Spirit can be called the actions, manifestations, or operations of the Holy Spirit in the lives of believers. As the Holy Spirit works in the believer, which He is in control of, several actions are evidenced or manifested in the life of that believer.

The Bible calls these the "gifts" or operations of the Holy Spirit. The Holy Spirit gives these gifts during His working in the believer so that God's purpose might be fulfilled, such as in witnessing, healing, speaking with unknown tongues (languages), miracles, administration, and so on. Read I Corinthians 12:7-11 to see all the gifts mentioned there for the benefit of the total body of Christ.

As we conclude this chapter, it is important that you note that the Holy Spirit is a gift of God to the believer to enable him or her to function adequately on Earth. The Christian has been given an assignment on Earth by God to do on behalf of Christ our King. God desiring us to do such an assignment well also provided us a Helper who is equal in strength and grace like our Lord Jesus Christ.

Therefore, every Christian who truly desires to

serve God completely has no choice whether he/she wants Him or desires to be filled by Him. For every Christian to faithfully and effectively do the work that God has given to us to do on Earth, we must receive and be filled with the Holy Spirit of God.

CHAPTER EIGHT

Move Forward & Grow In Christ

Jesus wants you, child of God, to move forward and grow in Him. The most important way that growth will come is through the study of God's Word. Therefore, it is most important that you establish a bible study habit early in your Christian walk. In this chapter, I want to help you lay some simple principles that will guide you throughout your walk with Christ.

Faith

The Bible defines faith for us according to Hebrews 11:1 - it says, "Now faith is the substance of things hoped for, the evidence of things not seen." In this definition lies the great victory for the believer and a key to walking with God. Your relationship with Christ is totally a work of grace by faith in

God. You were saved by grace through faith. All you did was to put your trust in God through the finished work of Christ and you became a child of God. Nothing more than that happened, at the point God changed you through Christ.

Faith In What God Says

Now remember that as a Christian, God speaks to you. The natural question is then, how does He speak? The primary way in which God speaks to His children is through the Bible. If you remember in chapter three (3), I shared with you how God speaks to us through sixty-six (66) books that we called the Old and New Testaments of the Bible. That is absolutely true. In the Bible, God communicates to you His promises, the direction for your life and His plans for eternity. The greatest growth that will take place in your life will come, as you believe what God says concerning you.

Your relationship with Christ calls for several commitments. There are three of them that I would like to examine. The first is intellectual, the second is emotional, and the final one is your will. Let us look at each separately.

Intellectual Commitment

It is an established fact that Jesus Christ came into this world to die for your sins and the sins of the whole world. It is a historical fact and many people witnessed His death, which satisfied the judgment and the wrath of God for mankind. It is on the basis of this that you can call yourself a child of God.

The New Testament that describes the total details of Jesus' fulfillment of God's plan for humanity was not written by some hired servants to put documents together, but by eyewitnesses who physically watched the crucifixion of the Lord. They watched Him buried and they saw Him after the resurrection. The Gospel of Luke and the book of Acts make this very clear. Listen to what the writer says concerning the record as he addresses the nobles and the learned of his days.

The Gospel of Luke – Chapter One

[1]For as much as many have taken in hand to set forth in order a declaration of those things which are most surely believed among us, [2]Even as they delivered them unto us, which from the beginning were eyewitnesses, and ministers of the word; [3]It

seemed good to me also, having had perfect understanding of all things from the very first, to write unto you in order, most excellent Theophilus, [4]That thou mightest know the certainty of those things, which thou hast been instructed.

This same Luke, a physician of repute, went on to write and address the same category of people in the book of Acts. Read what he said:

[1]The former treatise have I made O Theophilus, of all that Jesus began both to do and teach, [2]Until the day in which He was taken up, after He through the Holy Ghost had given commandments unto the apostles who He had chosen: [3]To whom also He showed Himself alive after His passion by many infallible proofs, being seen of them forty days and speaking of the things pertaining to the kingdom of God.

You can see from the record that the facts are as secure as any historical evidence can make it. Your commitment to the Word of God is guaranteed by the fact that the historical facts are true and can be depended upon. Jesus came, lived, died, and rose again for your redemption, reconciliation and restoration to God as His child. Therefore, you can trust the promises recorded in the word of God.

Emotional Commitment

Your walk with God towards maturity and taking your rightful place in Christ both involve your emotions or your feeling. However, it is important to know that all emotional expressions must be subject to facts of God's Word. Different people respond to situations differently because we are created uniquely by God. The inability to differentiate between all types of feelings or emotions has caused many people to confuse the reality of God dealing with them with fables.

As a Christian, do not base your faith on what happened to someone else, particularly if the Word of God does not verify it. In many cases it might agree with the Bible, but remember that God deals with each of us differently.

There will be times that you get up in the morning and you do not feel saved. Remember at that time, that your salvation is not based on how you feel, but rather on the finished work of Jesus Christ and God having been satisfied by the work Christ did to save you.

It is the same thing with the indwelling power and presence of the Holy Spirit. You will note that there are times when you will feel that you are filled with the Holy Spirit, as evidenced by your thoughts and your responses to situations. In those moments, remember that your feeling is subject to the authority of the Word of God.

Bear this in mind at all times. The assurance of your salvation and guarantee of your relationship with God is based on the authority of God's Word. The day you met the condition of God by putting your trust in the worthiness of Jesus Christ and not the unworthiness of yourself, God accepted you through Christ to become His child and nothing in this world can change that.

Also, as a child of God, He has made promises to you. The Bible shows us that God is a Keeper of His promises. Therefore, you can count on what He says. Understand this as a child of God, the greatest promise that God kept was that of sending Jesus Christ to die for our sins so that we could become the children of God. Now, if God did the greatest, why do you doubt that He can do the rest for you? To put it differently, if God saved you, do you think He will not take care of you?

This is what the Bible says concerning this, and you can bank your life on it. "What shall we then say to these things? If God be for us, who can be against us? He that spared not His own Son, but delivered Him up for us all, how shall He not with Him also freely give us all things?" (Romans 8:31-32)

On this matter, I do not know who can answer the questions raised here negatively. Therefore, you can raise your faith in God and His ability and commitment to keep His words to you. Do not depend on your feeling as you move forward to do exploits in God's great kingdom.

In conclusion of this particular section, let me emphasize that the facts about the Christian life are in the Bible. These facts do not change based on feeling, prevailing circumstances or situation. We know without doubt that our feelings change. What determines whether our feelings are up or down include what is happening at any given moment. Feelings, then, are subjective, while the facts of the Word of God are absolutely testable and constant.

The Commitment Of Your Will

In addition to our intellect and our emotions, being a child of God or becoming a Christian and moving forward to growth involves our will. Our commitment to obey what God says is carried out by us acting on our will. Jesus Christ knows this and during His earthly teachings He emphasized that in order to grow in God one must submit his/her will to the teachings of God and be able to test the same with their corresponding action. In John's gospel, He said:

> If any man will do His will, he shall know of the doctrine (teachings of Christ), whether it be of God, or whether I speak of myself. **John 7:17**

Basically, Christ is saying that unless you are willing to obey the truth you will never know the truth. Unless you are willing to follow what God says you will not grow to full maturity because moving to the next level involves your will.

Your willingness to walk in the light will cause you to pursue the light. If your will is not submitted to the Holy Spirit, the Spirit of God will not manifest Jesus to you the way He should because you have a choice to follow Him or not. The whole problem of man from the beginning has been that of letting God's will prevail, not because God wants to force His will upon us, but rather by our freely submitting our will to God as the caring Father and as one who has our great interest in His heart.

Now, as a Christian, knowing for a fact that you are a joint-heir with Jesus Christ, you are not a stranger to the inheritance of God in Christ, and the plans of God are not hidden from you. Thus, you can freely submit to God. The final result will be tremendous growth, which will allow the purpose of God for salvation to be accomplished in your life.

Remember, the plan of God for salvation was purposefully directed concerning you. To put it differently, salvation is a beginning of what God wants to accomplish in your life. God having saved you through Christ wants to make you an instrument of glory on earth. He wants you to function fully as His ambassador on Earth. However, you will not be able to fulfill your role as God's representative on earth unless you are growing and taking your rightful place in God's kingdom.

May you be greatly challenged to yield yourself to God so that He can use you and be glorified in your life.

Personal Growth Section

This section of study is for your personal growth and it is adapted from Billy Graham Evangelistic Association (BGEA) study material for Believers.
It is used by permission of both BGEA & InterVarsity Press.

We trust that is will be a blessing to you as you grow daily in Christ.

Growing In Christ

Knowing Christ

[1]Whether you have just become a Christian or are renewing your commitment to Christ, it's good to review some basic truths about Jesus Christ and the salvation He offers.

Our Need for Salvation

Though you may know many people who seem to be "better" than others, all of us make mistakes (Romans 3:23). The consequence of human sin and imperfection is eternal separation from God, who is holy and perfect. And since God is the very source of life, eternal separation from Him means eternal death (Romans 6:23).

Promise 1:
The Promise of Salvation

The Bible talks about "salvation," which means

being saved from eternal death and experiencing peace with God and living forever with Him. John 3:16, perhaps the best-known verse in the Bible, explains clearly that by believing in Jesus Christ you can have salvation and eternal life:

> For God so loved the world that he gave his one and only Son, that whoever believes in him shall not perish but have eternal life. **John 3:16**

Look at this verse, one phrase at a time, to better understand the simple truth it proclaims:

"For God so loved the world ..."

The "world" includes you and every other individual on the face of the earth. God loves you, and the next part of the verse shows just how much He loves you:

"... that he gave his one and only Son ..."

God loves you so much that He gave His Son (Romans 5:8). Jesus Christ, the Son of God, paid the penalty for your sins when He died on the cross. He took all your sins and died once for all. As He died He said, "It is finished" (John 19:30), meaning that He had truly done everything necessary for your salvation.

As the "Son of God," Jesus is equal to God Himself. He is part of what theologians call the "Trinity": God the Father, God the Son, and God the Holy Spirit. Amazingly, however, even though Jesus was equal to God the Father (John 1:1-3; 10:30), He freely chose to become a human being and die for us (Philippians 2:5-8).

"... that whoever believes in him shall not perish ..."

If you believe that Jesus Christ is God's Son, and accept Him as your Savior, you will not have to pay the eternal penalty for your sins—because Jesus paid that penalty for you when He died on the cross.

"... but have eternal life."

Instead of eternal death and separation from God, you will have eternal life the moment you trust Christ. You can know that:

- *your sins are forgiven (Colossians 1:14)*
- *you are a child of God (John 1:12)*
- *you possess eternal life (John 3:16)*

Committing Your Life to Jesus Christ

Have you personally trusted Jesus Christ as your Lord and Savior? If so, then on the authority of God's Word you have eternal life. If not, you can trust Him right now (Romans 10:13)! You can receive Jesus Christ into your life right now by praying a prayer such as this:

Dear Lord Jesus,

I know that I am a sinner and I need Your forgiveness. I believe that You died for my sins. I want to turn from my sins. I now invite You to come into my heart and life. I want to trust and follow You as Lord and Savior.

In Jesus' name, Amen.

Memorize John 3:16, and if you ever have occasion to doubt your salvation, use it as an anchor for your faith!

Promise 2:
The Promise of Victory Over Temptation

Satan does not want you to be in relationship with

God. He will concentrate on some area of spiritual weakness in your life to pull you down. Don't be surprised when this happens! Instead, learn to take your eyes off your own weaknesses and put your trust in Jesus Christ, who is able to help you. God promises you will not be tempted more than you can bear (1 Corinthians 10:13).

> *To overcome temptation, take the problem to God immediately, before it has a chance to take root. Be positive in your prayers. Don't concentrate on the thing that is tempting you, but think about godly things (Philippians 4:8).*

Ask God to bring such experiences and thoughts into your life. Meditate on 1 Corinthians 10:13 and rely on its promises whenever you are tempted.

Promise 3:
The Promise of Forgiveness

Learning to live the Christian life is like learning to walk. There will be many ups and downs, especially in the beginning (Psalm 37:23-24).

When you were learning to walk, you often fell

down. But did you stay down long? No, you reached out to the extended hand of your mother or father, who put you back on your feet. You can learn to walk with God the same way. When you fall, reach out to God through prayer, and accept His merciful helping hand:

> If we confess our sins, he is faithful and just and will forgive us our sins and purify us from all unrighteousness. **1 John 1:9**

Whenever you do something that displeases the Lord, as soon as the Spirit of God has made you aware of it, make things right with God. As you do this you will come to know—firsthand!—the mercy and forgiveness of God and the joy of being in constant fellowship with Him.

Memorize 1 John 1:9 and practice it daily. Take God at His Word and believe Him for forgiveness and cleansing.

Promise 4:
The Promise of His Presence

Because you are human, it will be natural for you to doubt, to be frustrated at times, and to feel weak

KNOWING CHRIST

and all alone. But you are never alone; Jesus Christ is in you and He wants to help you become the kind of person He created you to be (Philippians 1:6).

He will meet your every need and will take care of you daily (Hebrews 13:5). Jesus knew His followers' weaknesses and need for greater spiritual strength He wanted them to know that, even though He would not be present with them personally, the Holy Spirit, whom we have seen is a part of the Trinity, would take His place and meet their every need (John 14:16).

The Holy Spirit can be your Counselor or, as some Bible translations read, your "comforter." He can also be your teacher. As you read your Bible and ask God to help you understand it, the indwelling Spirit will guide you into the truth (John 16:13). He will also lead you (Romans 8:14), enrich your spiritual life (John 6:63; Romans 8:11), and empower you for Christian living (Galatians 5) and for dynamic witness to others about your faith (Acts 1:8).

The promises of salvation, of victory over temptation, of forgiveness, and of God's abiding presence are yours this very day. Practice God's presence, believe His promises, and walk in absolute dependence on His indwelling Holy Spirit.

Page 83

Your Response

Answer these questions by looking up the verses in the gospel of John:

1. What did Jesus come into the world to do? John 1:29

2. How did Jesus take away the sins of the world? John 19:16-18

3. God loved the world and gave His Son to die on the cross. John 3:16 tells how we can personally benefit from what God has done.

   (a) Fill in your first name in each of the following blank spaces: "For God loved _____ so much that He gave His only Son (Jesus) so that if _____ believes in Him, _____ will not perish (pay the penalty for sin), but _____ will have eternal life."

   (b) Physical life will end someday, but the life, which God wants to give each one of us, is eternal life—it will never end. What must you do to have eternal life? John 3:16

4. What new relationship do you now enjoy by believing in Christ? John 1:12

5. What happens to those who do not believe in Christ?

   (a) John 3:18

   (b) John 3:36

6. Eternal life is not obtained by being religious, keeping a set of rules, or doing good works, but by believing in a person, Jesus Christ. What does Jesus say in John 11:25-26?

7. What happens the moment you believe in Christ? John 5:24

8. Now, review your answers and state briefly how you know that your sins are forgiven and that you have eternal life:

Final Thought

Now that you have received Jesus Christ as your personal Lord and Savior, claim the assurance of your salvation. As a child needs physical food each day to grow, a child of God needs daily spiritual food.

1. Memorize these verses for Lesson 1.

Promise of Salvation: "For God so loved the world that he gave his one and only Son, that whoever believes in him shall not perish but have eternal life." **John 3:16**

Promise of Forgiveness: "If we confess our sins, he is faithful and just and will forgive us our sins and purify us from all unrighteousness." **1 John 1:9**

2. *Go on to the next lesson, "Growing in Christ."*

Growing In Christ

[1]God wants to meet with you personally—just you—each and every day.

That thought may amaze you, but consider it for a moment: When you accept Jesus Christ as Lord and Savior, you become a member of God's family, a child of God. You can call God your Father.

Any good parent wants to spend time with his or her children—sometimes with all of them together, but often with each one alone. That is how one person gets to know another person well—by spending time alone with that individual.

The best way to get to know your heavenly Father is to spend time alone with Him. You can do this each day by reading His Word and by talking with Him in prayer.

Listening to God: Reading His Word

How can a young man keep his way pure? By living

according to your word... I have hidden your word in my heart that I might not sin against you. **Psalm 119:9,11**

If you are just getting acquainted with the Bible, you will likely find the gospel of John the most interesting, because it sums up God's plan of salvation most beautifully.

After you have finished reading John, you may want to read the book of Acts to see how the early Christians shared their faith with those around them. Sharing your faith is one of the most important things you can do for God.

If you have not read much from the Bible, you may prefer to use a modern version. Ask your pastor or someone at your local Christian bookstore to recommend one.

While you are reading the Bible, meditate on what it says. To meditate simply means to think seriously about spiritual things. It means thinking quietly, soberly and deeply about God—how wonderful He is, what wonderful things He has done for you, what He is going to do for you, and what He wants you to do for Him.

As you read the Bible and meditate, perhaps you will notice:

- *a special promise to claim*

- *a principle to help you in your day*
- *a command you should follow*
- *a searchlight pointing out a sin or spiritual need in your life*
- *a meaningful verse to memorize*

Don't read too fast or try to finish too much at one time. To begin, a good rule of thumb is to read one chapter a day. Take time to look for all that God has for you in the day's passage. There's no need to rush through your time alone with God.

Talking to God: Prayer

This is the confidence we have in approaching God: that if we ask anything according to his will, he hears us. And if we know that he hears us— whatever we ask—we know that we have what we asked of him. **1 John 5:14-15**

After you have read and meditated awhile in God's Word, talk to Him in prayer. Talk to God as you would to a loving parent who wants the best for you and who wants to help you in every way possible.

You can pray to God any time of the day—driving to work, preparing dinner, washing clothes, studying at school. But you also need to find a time during your day when you can give the Lord your full attention, without any distractions.

Perhaps the morning is best for you—when you are fresh, before your active day begins. Or in the evening—at the close of the day, as you consider the next day's plans and prepare for a good night's rest. Better yet, try to spend some time alone with Him both morning and evening (Psalm 55:17)!

Whatever the time of day, be consistent in your meeting with God. Jesus rose early to pray, and He went somewhere that was quiet (Luke 5:16).

A Prayer Guide

These suggestions may help you know how to start talking to God:

- *Praise Him for who He is—Creator and Sustainer of the entire universe, yet interested in you personally!*

- *Thank Him for all He has done, for all He is doing for you, and for all He has promised to do for you.*

- *Admit to Him the things you have done or said or thought for which you are sorry. God is both willing and able to forgive our sins (1 John 1:9).*

- *Pray for your family.*
- *Pray for others—for friends or neighbors who have needs, both physical and spiritual.*
- *Pray for yourself. Ask God's guidance for the day. Ask Him to help you with any problem you have. Ask Him to give you opportunities to serve Him.*

Try listing your prayer requests, so that you don't forget any, and so you can record God's answers. (He may say "yes," or "no," or "wait"!) Keep your list in a small notebook or on 3" x 5" cards—something small enough to fit in your pocket or billfold or purse.

Remember, you can pray to the Lord any time, anywhere, and about anything—to ask for something you need or to thank Him for something you have received. As any loving earthly father would be, God is interested in all that happens to you.

He is looking forward to His time alone with you!

Your Response

God speaks to us through the Bible, and we in

THE BELIEVER'S GROWTH MANUAL

turn can speak to Him through prayer. As we carry on this dialogue, we become better acquainted with His glorious promises and blessings. This lesson should make Bible reading and prayer more meaningful.

1. Turn to the following passages in John's gospel, and briefly summarize the statements Jesus made about Himself.

   (a) John 6:35

   (b) John 8:12

   (c) John 10:9

   (d) John 11:25-26

2. What does Jesus promise if you keep His commandments? John 14:21

3. What further help is promised in John 14:26?

4. What does Jesus ask you to do in John 13:34-35, and why?

   (a) What does He ask you to do? v. 34

   (b) Why? v. 35

5. Read John 21:1-6. Describe what happened in verses 3 and 6.

(a) v. 3

(b) v. 6

(c) What important lesson can you learn from these verses?

(d) What similar truth is taught in John 15:5?

6. As a believer, what is now your privilege? John 16:24

7. As you grow in Christ, your faith and confidence will increase, and you will pray with greater assurance. What are you promised in John 15:16?

Final Thought

God, the Holy Spirit, is your teacher, and He uses the Scriptures to teach you. As you continue to read, study and memorize the Scriptures—and pray—Christ will become more real and you will find fulfillment in life.

1. Memorize these verses for Lesson 2.

Confidence in Prayer: "This is the confidence we have in approaching God: that if we ask anything according to his will, he hears us. And if we know that he hears us—whatever we ask—we know that we have what we asked of him." **1 John 5:14-15**

Victory through God's Word: "How can a young man keep his way pure? By living according to your word. ... I have hidden your word in my heart that I might not sin against you." **Psalm 119: 9,11**

2. *Please continue now to the next lesson, "Obeying Christ."*

LESSON 3
Obeying Christ

²As you grow as a new Christian, you will find that true contentment and fulfillment comes in surrendering complete control of your life to Jesus Christ. This means letting Him have highest authority over your life, as King and Lord.

Being a Christian is not just worshipping God for an hour on Sunday. A true follower of Jesus Christ is committed to a life of obedience to Him, 24/7, for the rest of his or her life. And it is a full life and an exciting adventure (John 10:10)!

Making Jesus Christ your Lord—living a lifestyle of obedience and dependence on Christ—brings about changes in the way you live.

Live Wholeheartedly

First, living with Jesus Christ as your Lord is a wholehearted way of life. We are called to serve God with all our hearts! Wholehearted followers are what

God is looking for (2 Chronicles 16:9). Surrender your heart each day to Him, ready and willing to be like Him and serve the King of your life (Ephesians 6:7).

A Relationship of Love

Second, living with Jesus Christ as your Lord is a relationship of love. Your love for God is expressed through obedience (Matthew 22:37-40). Love is more than a feeling—it's something we do. When you love your King, you obey His commands (John 14:21).

Obedience relates to every aspect of our lives: relationships with family and friends, our jobs, career plans and future ambitions—everything must be surrendered to God's plans. We need to care more about what God thinks about us than what people think. Our bank accounts, possessions, time and everything we claim as ours, must be under God's control. Even our social life and leisure time should be yielded to Christ.

Be willing to obey Christ even when there is personal cost involved (Luke 14:33).

Through obedience to Christ, we come to really know Him, and we become more like Him. Jesus makes Himself real to us.

Run to Obtain the Prize

Third, living with Jesus Christ as your Lord means living a focused life aimed at glorifying God. God has a plan for each of our lives. Fulfilling these plans involves our active, disciplined effort. The Apostle Paul described the Christian life as an Olympic competition. In the same way that an Olympic athlete devotes him or herself to rigorous training, so we are challenged to work at our relationship with Christ, growing in our understanding of God's Word, developing our character to be more like Christ, and living by Christ's example (1 Corinthians 9:24).

What we do with the 24 hours we are given each day determines the effectiveness of our Christian life and our service for Christ. God calls us to be productive believers, bearing "fruit" for God. Like a branch that draws life-giving sap from the vine, we draw our sustenance from union with Christ, and recognize our dependence on Him (John 15:5). That's how we live our lives in a way that pleases God (1 Corinthians 10:31).

Be Transformed

Finally, living with Jesus Christ as Lord of our lives

is a life of transformation. We can't live perfect lives. When we fail, we can bring those failures to Jesus Christ. He promises to forgive and cleanse us (1 John 1:9). Every day we need to let go of the old way of living and remember we are new creations (Ephesians 4:24). By turning away from our sins and receiving the new life Christ gave us, we steadily become more like Him (Romans 12:2).

The Christian life often runs against the current of the world around us. So we need wholehearted commitment, true love for Jesus Christ, a disciplined lifestyle and readiness to admit our failures and leave behind our old ways of living in order to live victoriously in Christ. By surrendering to Jesus Christ in every area of our lives, we can live life to its fullest as He intended.

Your Response

Living life abundantly—is it really possible? Is Jesus calling us to follow Him in obedience just to make us good, moral people, or is He really trying to show us the true pathway to joy? Are you ready to trust the leadership of the Good Shepherd and make Jesus the Lord of your life? Perhaps the following questions will help you understand more about the joy of truly surrendering your life to God's control.

1. Study 1 Corinthians 6:19-20 and answer three important questions concerning Christ's lordship over your life:

    (a) Now that you are a Christian, what has your body become?

    (b) Why do you now belong to Christ?

    (c) What should now be your purpose in life?

2. Read Luke 6:46-49 and briefly summarize what you think Jesus was teaching in the parable of the wise and foolish builders:

    (a) What must we do if we call Jesus our Lord?

    (b) What spiritual truth is represented by the house built on the rock?

    (c) What spiritual truth is represented by the house with no foundation?

3. What does the apostle James say about obeying the Bible? James 1:22-25

4. Obedience to Jesus Christ as Lord is the true test of your commitment to Him. What does

the apostle John say about obedience? Find one thing in each verse. 1 John 2:3-6

5. What is another sure way of knowing you belong to Christ? 1 John 3:14

6. As you grow in Christ, there will be times when you fail Him. No one except Christ has ever lived a perfect life. Be willing to admit you have failed and confess your sin. Briefly summarize what each verse in 1 John 1:8-10 teaches about confession and forgiveness.

7. What can you thank God for right now, concerning your need for God's forgiveness? 1 John 2:1-2

Final Thought

1. Memorize these verses for Lesson 3:

Applying God's Word: "Do not let this Book of the Law depart from your mouth; meditate on it day and night, so that you may be careful to do everything written in it. Then you will be prosperous and successful." **Joshua 1:8**

Confirmation of My Love for God: "Whoever has my commands and obeys them, he is the one who loves me. He who loves me will be loved by my Father, and I too will love him and show myself to him." **John 14:21**

2. *Please continue now to your final lesson. This could be the most important lesson of all. It concerns sharing your faith with others.*

Witnessing For Christ

[1]A witness in a courtroom tells what he or she knows about a given situation. The Christian witness tells others what he or she knows about Jesus Christ and what it means to personally trust Him with his or her life.

When He began His ministry, Jesus called two fishermen, Simon Peter and his brother Andrew, and said, "Come, follow me ... and I will make you fishers of men" (Matthew 4:19). Through the ages, the same call has gone out to all those who put their faith in Jesus Christ. He reaches others through the faithful witness of people like you (2 Corinthians 5:19-20).

Your Life Example

As a witness for Christ, your life is a key part of your witness. You are a new creation—the way your new faith shows itself in your conduct is the greatest testimony you have (Matthew 5:16). This means your habits and lifestyle should reflect a life given over to Jesus Christ. It does not mean that you must be perfect before you can be a witness. We all stumble from time to time as we are learning to walk, but as you learned in Lesson 1, God is willing to forgive your sins and put you back on your feet again.

The Power of the Holy Spirit

You also need a power beyond yourself in order to witness—this is the Holy Spirit. Jesus promises that the Holy Spirit will give us power to tell others about Him (Acts 1:8). When your life is clean and you walk under the control of the Holy Spirit, He is able to witness through you.

A man named Philip was chosen to serve the church because he was "full of the Spirit and wisdom" (Acts 6:3). He was having a successful ministry in Samaria (Acts 8:4-13), when an angel summoned him to go to Gaza (Acts 8:26), where an Ethiopian official was returning from Jerusalem. The Ethiopian was reading from chapter 53 of Isaiah at the time.

Empowered by the Holy Spirit, Philip began to talk with the Ethiopian using that very passage of Scripture and telling him the good news about Jesus (Acts 8:35).

The Power of God's Word

The third critical ingredient to effective witness is God's Word—the Bible. In the story of Philip, God put the appropriate Scripture in the hands of the Ethiopian before He sent Philip to share with him. When the seed of God's Word is planted in a prepared heart, it produces fruit—a new believer in Christ (I Peter 1:23).

It's exciting to share your newfound faith in Jesus Christ with others. A great way to start is to tell how Jesus Christ changed your own life. There is great power in a simple and honest personal testimony. Also, be prepared with the facts of the Gospel message in mind.

Sharing Your Faith

When you are explaining the Gospel it may help to draw it on paper for the friend with whom you are sharing.

Step 1: Explain the facts.

On the top of your page list the four basic truths of the Gospel (see "Steps to Peace with God"). List them one at a time and use a Scripture or two with each one.

Draw the graphic of God on one side of the chasm and us on the other. As you draw, share Bible verses that explain how the separation took place. Show how the cross bridges the chasm between God and us and how we can cross the bridge through faith in Christ.

Step 2: Invite a response.

If you feel led by the Holy Spirit and the person is responding positively, offer an invitation, such as, "If this illustration is true—and I believe with all my heart that it is—then all of us are on either one side of the chasm or the other."

Then ask, "Which side are you on? Here ... or here?" If your friend is unsure or knows he or she is on the wrong side, your friend can be sure of his or her position by:

1. Admitting your need—that you are a sinner

2. Being willing to turn away from your sins

3. Believing that Jesus Christ died for you on the Cross and rose from the grave.

4. Praying to invite Jesus Christ to be the Lord and Savior of your life and control your life through the Holy Spirit.

Step 3: Pray with the person responding.

Everyone who calls on the name of the Lord will be saved (Romans 10:13). Remember, Jesus Christ is the door to eternal life. Through prayer we can enter that door and receive Him as Lord and Savior. Lead the person in a simple prayer, such as:

"Dear Lord Jesus, I know that I am a sinner and need Your forgiveness. I believe that You died for my sins. I want to turn from my sins. I now invite You to come into my heart and life. I want to trust and follow You as Lord and Savior. In Jesus' name. Amen."

Step 4: Confirm the new believer in his or her decision.

If your friend sincerely prays that prayer, he or she has become a Christian and has been saved from eternal death! You will want to share some Bible verses (such as 1 John 5:12-13) to give your friend assurance of his or her new standing before God.

Follow-up

When you help a person in coming to faith in Christ, remember that this individual is a spiritual baby (1 Peter 2:2). In order to grow, an infant needs nurture and care. This means encouraging the person to begin to read the Bible and pray regularly. You can do so by using this online Bible study. Share what you have learned from "Living in Christ." Also encourage this new Christian to find a Bible-teaching church in order to have fellowship with other believers in Christ and continue to grow.

A witness in a courtroom tells what he or she knows about a given situation. The Christian witness tells others what he or she knows about Jesus Christ and what it means to personally trust Him.

1. What is the Good News (Gospel) that we should share? 1 Corinthians 15:1-4

2. What power does the Gospel possess? Romans 1:16

3. What are three things an effective witness for Christ must have?

   (a) Matthew 5:16

   (b) Acts 1:8

   (c) 1 Peter 1:22-23

4. Review Lesson 3 on witnessing and briefly explain the "Bridge to Life" illustration.

5. Once a person is convinced of his or her sin and need of a Savior, what should that person do?

   (a) Acts 3:19

   (b) John 10:9

   (c) John 1:12

6. When a person believes in Jesus Christ, what can he or she now say with assurance? John 3:16

Your Response

A witness in a courtroom tells what he or she knows about a given situation. The Christian witness tells others what he or she knows about Jesus Christ and what it means to personally trust Him.

1. What is the Good News (Gospel) that we should share? 1 Corinthians 15:1-4

2. What power does the Gospel possess? Romans 1:16

3. What are three things an effective witness for Christ must have?

   (a) Matthew 5:16

(b) Acts 1:8

(c) 1 Peter 1:22-23

4. Review Lesson 3 on witnessing and briefly explain the "Bridge to Life" illustration.

5. Once a person is convinced of his or her sin and need of a Savior, what should that person do?

(a) Acts 3:19

(b) John 10:9

(c) John 1:12

6. When a person believes in Jesus Christ, what can he or she now say with assurance? John 3:16.

Final Thought

Memorize these verses for Lesson 4.

Telling Others about Christ: "But you will receive power when the Holy Spirit comes on you; and you will be my witnesses in Jerusalem, and in all Judea and Samaria, and to the ends of the earth" (Acts 1:8).

"Come, follow me," Jesus said, "and I will make you fishers of men" (Matthew 4:19).

Permissions:

ISBN 0-9748875-0-1